WILDLIFE in DANGER

Malcolm Penny

Illustrated by Bill Donohoe

SIMON & SCHUSTER
LONDON • SYDNEY • NEW YORK • TOKYO • SINGAPORE • TORONTO

Contents

Introduction 5

1. **Whales and Whaling**
   The Whaling Trade 6
   Saving the Whales 8

2. **Seals and Sealskin**
   The Seal Slaughter 10
   Saving their Skins 12

3. **The Fur Trade**
   Killing for Fur 14
   Is Fur Fashionable? 16

4. **Trading in Animals**
   The Animal Smugglers 18
   Stop the Trade 20

5. **Pointless Slaughter**
   Killing without Cause 22
   Saving the Innocent 24

6. **Polluting the Planet**
   Pollution and Acid Rain 26
   Fighting Pollution 28

7. **Rainforests**
   Rainforest Destruction 30
   Preserving the Rainforests 32

8. **Wetlands under Threat**
   Vanishing Wetlands 34
   Protecting Wetlands 36

9. **Endangered Plants**
   Plants under Threat 38
   Planting the Future 40

Glossary 42
Further Information 43
Index 44

Introduction

When human beings first evolved, they had no more impact on their environment than any other middle-sized omnivorous animal. Small bands of upright apes roamed the plains, but they were probably eaten as prey just as often as they caught and ate other animals. Later, *Homo sapiens* was to become the dominant species on earth.

At first the new species hunted animals and gathered plants to eat; later it learned to grow food plants. Over the centuries villages grew into cities, coal and the oil replaced wood as the main fuel, and horses gave way to machines. People rejoiced in their progress.

The greatest progress was in the growth of the human species. The population grew so rapidly that there came a time when people realized that they were in danger of overwhelming all the other living things on earth. That time is now.

The danger comes from pollution, over-hunting, the spreading of the deserts and the destruction of the remaining wilderness.

Although the situation is serious, it is not too late. In this book we shall consider what can be done to prevent the other animals and plants in the world that we have mastered dying out because of our activities.

A harp seal pup in Newfoundland, Canada. Baby harp seals and fur seals are two of the species that are killed for their soft skins.

WHALES AND WHALING — 1

The Whaling Trade

People began hunting whales from small open boats at least a thousand years ago. One whale would provide food, oil and bone for a large number of people. Such small-scale hunting, in which whales were killed one at a time, did no harm to whale populations. The damage was done when whaling became a large-scale commercial operation, carried out for profit.

Commercial whaling
At first, the commercial whalers also used small boats, and the same simple spears and lances as their predecessors. It was a dangerous trade. It was also very profitable, and soon developed from a trade into an industry.

Now, fast ships are used to chase whales, which are killed with exploding harpoons fired from guns. The bodies are brought back to a factory ship, where oil and whalebone are removed, and the meat is then frozen.

A minke whale is cut up on board a Japanese factory ship.

Even with modern methods, whaling is very cruel. Unless a lucky shot hits the brain, an exploding harpoon can take anything up to half an hour to kill a whale, which dies by drowning in its own blood.

In the past, the main products of whaling were oil for lighting and machines, and whalebone (baleen), used to stiffen corsets. Later, mineral oils and plastics replaced them. Now, meat is the main product, with Japan as the major consumer. Sperm whale oil is still said to be the best lubricant for automatic gearboxes in cars, although scientists have recently discovered that the oil from the jojoba plant is just as good. Minor whale products include ambergris, which is used in the perfume industry, and sperm whale teeth, used as ornaments.

Declining numbers

Thirty thousand whales were killed in 1933 and the numbers rose to a peak in the 1960s. They then began to decline. In 1962, 67,000 were killed, but even by 1972 the whalers were still managing to find well over 40,000 whales to kill every year.

One reason for the decline in the catch was that whales became so scarce that it was hardly worthwhile hunting them. Some of them came very close to extinction. Now there may be only about 1,000 blue whales and 4,000 humpbacks left in Antarctic waters. Before whaling began, there were about 250,000 blues, and as many as 300,000 humpbacks. The number of fin whales has fallen in only fifteen years from 100,000 to around 4,000.

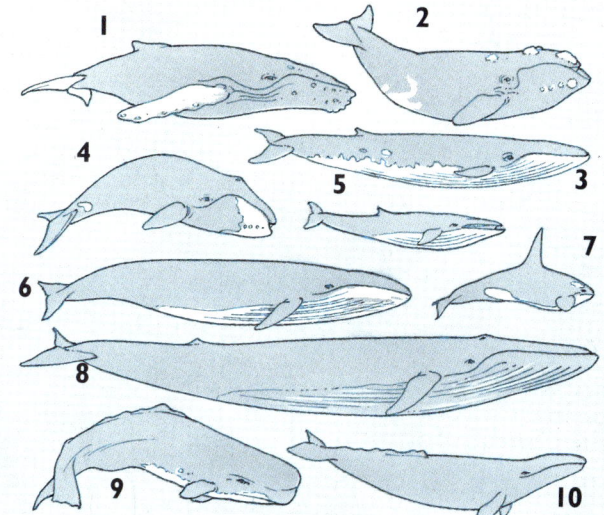

Threatened whale species: 1. Humpback; 2. Great Right; 3. Sei; 4. Bowhead; 5. Minke; 6. Fin; 7. Great Killer; 8. Blue; 9. Great Sperm; 10. Grey.

WHALES AND WHALING — 2

Saving the Whales

The first attempt to control the killing of whales was in 1948, when the fourteen whaling countries formed the International Whaling Commission (IWC). Its members agreed to meet at the start of each whaling season, to decide on the 'quota' of whales for the year. This meant that they estimated how many whales the population could afford to lose, fixed a starting date for the season, and agreed that they would all stop killing when the quota had been reached.

The result was that more whales were killed after the IWC was set up than before, as each member country raced to grab as many as it could before the season came to an end. Many of them ignored the quota rule altogether.

The whaling moratorium

In 1972 things began to change. The United Nations agreed that there should be a moratorium on whaling; that is, that it should be stopped completely for ten years. The IWC voted by a narrow majority to carry on whaling, but eventually the balance of influence within the IWC was changed. A halt on commercial whaling to begin in the 1985-86 season was agreed, to be reviewed in the summer of 1990. However, some countries—Japan, Norway and the USSR—objected to the ban and carried on as before, although the USSR has now given up commercial whaling.

Another country, Iceland, led the way in using a loophole in the IWC regulations. This allowed

Greenpeace members sail close to a Russian whaling ship but are unable to save the whale it has hunted and harpooned.

Anti-whaling protesters outside a meeting of the International Whaling Commission.

whales to be killed for scientific research. However, in 1989 Iceland announced that it would stop killing for science. Japan and Norway still carry on – awaiting the review of the commercial whaling ban.

One cause of the change in public opinion that led to the ban on whaling was the action of Greenpeace, an organization devoted to saving wildlife and the environment all over the world. Its members sailed between whaling ships and their prey in small rubber boats, daring them to fire their harpoons with the world watching on television. There were several unpleasant incidents, and many whales were killed in spite of the action, but people all over the world saw what was happening and took Greenpeace's side in the argument.

When the ban on whaling is reviewed, we may hope that enough proper scientific research has been done to enable us to tell how many whales are really left, and what would be the effect of continuing to kill them.

What you can do
Read the newspapers, and make sure that people around you know what is going on; write to your MP if you disagree with the Government's plans after the moratorium is reviewed. Support the work of Greenpeace, and other groups campaigning against whaling.

SEALS AND SEALSKIN — 1

The Seal Slaughter

In the past, at the same time as whales were being killed, sealers were killing seals, partly for their oil, and partly for their skins. The trade nearly came to an end when the seals were almost completely wiped out, but it continued in one or two places, in a particularly nasty form. Although the skin of fur seals went out of fashion, there was still a market for the silky skins of baby seals, especially harp and hooded seals from North America and Norway.

Baby seals are extremely easy to kill because they lie with their mothers where they are born, in large groups on favourite beaches. The sealers have only to walk up to the helpless babies and kill them by hitting them on the head with a club. They do this to avoid spoiling the skin by making a hole in it, as a bullet would do.

Dramatic decline

The mother seals give birth to just one baby each year, and only if they are left undisturbed. If the babies are killed each year, with all the disturbance that that causes, the mothers often fail to mate in time to have a baby the following year. This causes the population to fall very quickly. The result of killing the babies has been to reduce the seal populations in the main hunting areas to a third of what they were before, from 9 million to around 3 million.

Reducing the population is the aim of another seal-killing operation, the so-called 'cull' of grey seals around the European coasts. Fishermen believe that their catches are getting smaller because seals eat too many fish, and so they set out

These hunters have slaughtered a harp seal on the ice near the coast of Newfoundland, in eastern Canada. The sea is coloured dark red by the seal's blood.

to kill a certain number of them every year. Until 1988 this was permitted by law in selected places in Europe; but the outbreak of seal distemper, a virus which killed nearly 18,000 common seals and a few greys in northern Europe, caused the authorities to think again, and in 1988 the cull was cancelled.

Scientists were puzzled by the sudden outbreak of the disease. Although it seemed similar to the distemper which affects dogs, it was caused by a different virus. Nobody could suggest where it had come from, or why it affected common seals so badly. Then there were reports that seals in the Baltic and the North Sea were losing their resistance to other diseases, and there was some evidence that this was caused by pollution. No one yet knows the truth, but it is a cause for great concern.

Commercial fishing

The activities of commercial fishermen off the coast of Norway have damaged seals in another way. Fish stocks in the North Sea have fallen sharply in recent years, probably because of overfishing. Every year thousands of harp seals swim closer than usual to the shore to look for food. They find themselves trapped in the fishermen's nets, where they drown.

Fur seals are clubbed to death because shooting would leave holes in the skins, making them less valuable.

The distribution of two of the main species of seal around the Arctic.

 Harp seals

Northern fur seals

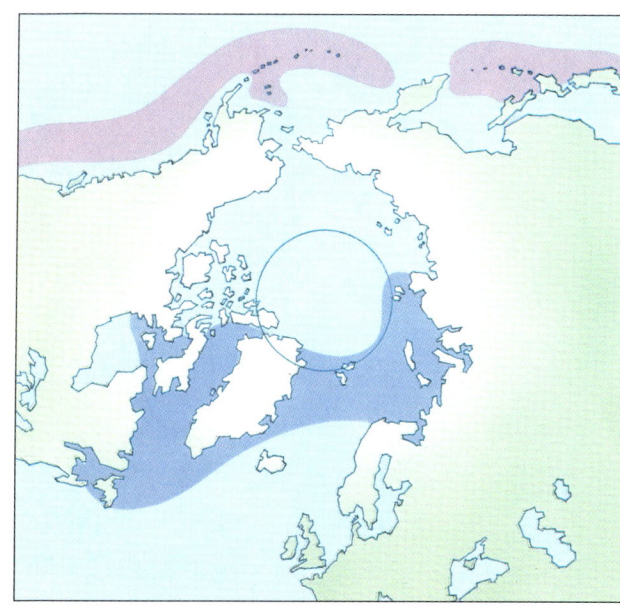

SEALS AND SEALSKINS — 2

Saving their Skins

Not very long ago, young girls used to have little purses made of silky, silver sealskin. However, when newspapers printed pictures showing how the baby seals were killed, and television programmes showed the hunt in all its gory reality, public opinion changed. Most people stopped buying the purses in the 1960s, and in 1983 the import of sealskin was banned in all the countries of the European Community. The ban took effect at once. Baby seals are still killed for their skins in Norway and in parts of Canada, but the skins cannot be imported into the European Community. The cull of adults goes on, too, in several places. The excuse given for the killing is that the seals eat too many fish. But the real reason that fish catches are falling in many parts of the world is that fishermen are catching too many small fish before they can grow big enough to breed and replenish their numbers.

Brian Davies, the founder of IFAW, first told the gory truth about the killing of seals.

Action by IFAW

The International Fund for Animal Welfare was one of the groups that helped to bring about the ban on sealskin imports into Europe. They did this not only by showing people what the hunt involved, but also by going out to the sealing grounds to stand between the sealers and their quarry. They saved some seal pups by spraying them with a harmless dye which made their skins worthless to the hunters.

What you can do
Never buy souvenirs or toys made from sealskin: they are still available in Canada and some non-EC countries. Tell the shopkeeper that you will not buy them and why. Support the International Fund for Animal Welfare and other groups fighting against sealing.

The fish farming solution
One answer to declining catches is to breed fish in captivity. One of the most commonly farmed fish is salmon. They are held inside a large net, often in a small bay of the sea. Outside the main net, which has a small mesh, is another with a much larger mesh. The outer net is supposed to keep seals from catching the fish; but when tides and currents push the two nets together the seals can bit a hole in the inner net, so that the salmon escape. Then the seals eat them. For 'doing what comes naturally' many seals are shot by fish farmers. But correctly designed nets exist to prevent seals from taking fish.

THE FUR TRADE — 1

Killing for Fur

In the past people wore fur as a necessity, to keep warm. But in recent years fur has become a luxury, worn only by the rich. Spotted and striped cats, such as leopards, cheetahs, and even tigers, were killed, and their skins used to make expensive coats. Smaller animals such as mink and beavers were trapped for the same trade. Many of the animals became very rare as a result. Ocelots, chinchillas and jaguars in South America, and bears, bobcats and lynx in North America, for example, are now scarce because of the fashion for wearing fur.

It is hard to understand how people who have pet cats and dogs can happily put on a coat made from the skins of other small animals. Perhaps they have no idea how the animals are caught.

In the old days the trapper, trudging through the snowy forests in his deerskin clothes and fur hat, was thought of as a brave, tough man. When he returned to the trading post with a bundle of rich, soft skins, he could earn a lot of money. The men who bought and sold the skins afterwards made even more. People preferred not to think about what happened when a wild animal was trapped, killed and skinned.

Furs are auctioned in a street in Anchorage, Alaska, USA.

Types of trap

The most common traps are either snares or leghold traps (often called 'gins'). A snare is a piece of wire with a loop in the end, which strangles an animal that puts its head through it. It can take an animal a long time to die, especially if it is caught by a leg or round the body.

A gin trap is intended to catch an animal's leg between two steel jaws, which are snapped shut by a spring when the victim steps on a metal plate between them. Animals have been known to chew their own legs off to escape from a trap. Gin traps have been illegal in Britain since the 1950s, though skins from animals caught with them in other countries can still legally be imported.

Both these types of trap, together with cage traps and pitfalls, are very cruel, because the animal suffers great pain and a slow death. However, they are still used today in many parts of the world to catch animals for the fur trade.

THE FUR TRADE — 2

Is Fur Fashionable?

Fur coats are becoming unfashionable, as people realize the cruelty involved in killing the animals to make them. In the 1970s campaigns were run to make people ashamed of wearing fur coats. Sometimes ink was thrown over them and some conservation organizations, such as the Wildfowl and Wetlands Trust, refused to admit people who were wearing the skin of a striped or spotted cat. However, in spite of the change in public opinion, governments have been slow to change the law to make the use of wild-trapped fur illegal.

The fur trade

The reasons for this are complicated, but easy to understand in one way: the fur trade is worth a lot of money to a lot of people. For the hunters and traders, fur is often their only source of income; and for the makers and sellers of fur coats, the profits are enormous. Both groups have put pressure on their governments to stop the law being changed.

The trade is becoming smaller, all the same, partly because the animals are harder to find and partly because fewer people now want to buy fur. A survey in 1988 found that seven out of every ten people in Britain thought that it was wrong to kill animals for their fur. In 1990 the famous Harrods store in London closed down its fur department.

Farmed fur

Nowadays only 13 per cent of the fur used to make clothing comes from wild-trapped animals. The rest comes from animals that have been bred in captivity. This is called 'farmed', or 'ranched', fur. Whether or not to buy such fur is a matter for each person's conscience, like deciding whether or not to eat meat.

However, although many people say that we need to eat some meat to stay healthy, nobody can claim that wearing fur is necessary. Modern fabrics are just as warm, much lighter and easier to keep clean, as well as being a lot cheaper. It is even possible to make fake fur that looks just like the real thing.

An organization called Lynx, which was founded in Britain in 1985, campaigns to persuade people not to wear fur of any kind. The international organization CITES (see page 20) has also worked hard to try to stop the fur trade between countries.

As a result of these protests, some species of animals killed for fur in the past have now made a good recovery. Sea otters in Alaska and California, and fur seals in the North Sea and the Antarctic, which were both hunted nearly to extinction in the nineteenth century, have begun to increase in number since the fur hunters left them alone.

As well as being cheaper and easier to keep clean, fake fur is just as beautiful as the real thing. Coats like this are now accepted in the world of fashion.

Farming mink is one alternative to trapping them in the wild. But should they live and die just to make expensive fur coats?

Hard-hitting adverts like this one have helped to change public attitudes to wearing fur.

> **What you can do**
> Politely tell people wearing fur clothes why you would not wear them yourself. Explain that even captive-bred fur involves cruelty to animals. Support Lynx, and other anti-fur trade groups.

17

TRADING IN ANIMALS — 1

The Animal Smugglers

There are people all over the world who will buy live exotic animals to keep in captivity. Some of the animals have become very rare in the wild, often just because so many of them have been trapped for collectors. All kinds of animals are involved, from frogs to brightly coloured birds, and from butterflies to rare mammals. The trade is worth billions of pounds a year.

Many of the animals involved in the trade die. It does not matter to the people who pack them for their journey if only a few survive. Small birds are packed in tiny cages, parrots are hidden in suitcases, and falcons in the spare wheel compartments of cars. Tortoises are crammed by the hundred into large boxes and very few arrive alive. Fish are often very valuable to collectors, and are treated with more care. Fish from Lake Malawi are transplanted in plastic bags blown up with extra oxygen. Overall, it is the developing world that supplies the wildlife, and the developed world that consumes it.

There is also a steady and illegal trade in animal products, such as ivory from elephant's tusks, and

The black rhino has been hunted almost to extinction. Its horn is used for traditional medicines, but mostly for the handles of ceremonial daggers in North Yemen.

18

Just the tip of the iceberg
These are only some of the creatures killed or traded each year. There are many others.
- 45,000 elephants from Africa
- 2,000-3,000 rhinos from Africa and Asia
- 7 million wild birds, including 500,000 parrots, worldwide
- several million butterflies from South-East Asia
- 150,000 spotted cats from South America and Central Africa
- 60,000 apes from Central Africa and South-East Asia

rhino horn, which is supposed to have medicinal properties. Souvenir hunters often buy grotesque trophies of their visits to foreign countries, such as gorilla heads and hands, or lion skins.

Ivory hunters

In 1981 there were over 480,000 elephants in East Africa. Today, because of the ivory trade, the number is down to about 150,000 and falling. In Kenya elephant poachers work in gangs of up to fifteen men, half of them armed with automatic weapons and the rest acting as carriers. They travel on foot or in Land-Rovers, venturing into the national parks where hunting is illegal. Often whole elephant families, numbering a dozen or more, are gunned down and their tusks hacked from them with axes or chainsaws.

Dealers buy the tusks from the poachers and the haul then passes through traders in ports to be smuggled abroad. As many as a dozen big-time dealers might be involved. Most African ivory is taken to Japan and Hong Kong, where it is carved into ornaments and exported all over the world.

TRADING IN ANIMALS — 2

Stop the Trade

The trapping and killing of endangered animals can be prevented either by defending the animals themselves or by trying to stop the trade. Trade in rare animals is monitored by an organization called the Convention on the International Trade in Endangered Species (CITES), which has 102 member countries. Under CITES, countries have to report how many rare animals they export. Animals on the list called Appendix I may not be traded at all, and trade in Appendix II animals must be strictly controlled. The black rhino is on Appendix I.

An example of an Appendix II animal is the colobus monkey, whose beautiful black and white fur was once used in the fashion trade. In the 1970s about 20,000 skins were exported from Kenya every year. But after Kenya joined CITES the highest number recorded in any one year between 1980 and 1985 was 314.

Fossey and the gorillas

One person who fought against poaching was Dian Fossey. She made her home in the Virunga National Park in Rwanda, Africa, where she studied, befriended and protected a group of highly endangered mountain gorillas. Her favourite gorilla, Digit, was a young orphan and for thirteen years they lived side by side. Then, in 1977, Digit was killed by poachers and his head and hands were hacked from his body for souvenirs.

Rwanda is a poor country, and poverty turns many people to poaching. Although it is illegal the trade offers a way of earning money for food. Digit's death hardened Fossey's determination to combat

Dian Fossey with two orphaned young mountain gorillas. She devoted her life to them until her murder in 1985.

Farming a solution

Crocodiles have been hunted for their skins to such an extent that many species are on the verge of extinction. One solution is crocodile farming, now widespread in many countries. In Papua New Guinea local hunters are encouraged to bring small living crocodiles to the farm where they are reared and 'harvested'. In under five years exports of farmed skins have grown to 10 per cent of the total trade. A crocodile breeding programme is also being developed.

The farming of wildlife takes pressure off the wild population, and many farms release adults back into the wild. But there may be a drawback: some people think farming will create a bigger demand and encourage more poaching.

Below Feeding time at a crocodile farm.

the poachers, and she introduced effective anti-poaching patrols in the Park. Then, eight years after Digit's death, Fossey herself was murdered in her cottage. To this day no one knows if poachers were responsible. But her work lives on; a fund she established in Digit's memory continues to finance anti-poaching patrols. The gorillas that remain owe their survival to Dian Fossey's efforts.

What you can do

If you visit a foreign country don't buy goods made from wild animals or birds, and don't buy or gather any wild plants as they may be endangered species. Likewise, at home don't buy or accept anything made from wildlife, especially ivory.

POINTLESS SLAUGHTER — 1

Killing without Cause

Some of the world's largest animals are rare now because they have been hunted for sport, or because they are treated as worthless. Between about 1880 and 1940, it was fashionable to go 'big-game hunting': that is, shooting large animals for fun. Rhinos, lions, zebras and even giraffes were killed, and their bodies carried home as trophies.

In India, the Maharajahs and their British guests hunted tigers. In 1939, after fifty years of hunting, there were between 20,000 and 30,000 tigers in India, but by 1972 there were only 1,827 left. The hunters shot every tiger they could find; the Maharajah of Sarguja held the record, with a lifetime 'bag' of 1,150 tigers.

Fox hunting is a social occasion in rural areas of Britain. Opponents argue that it is a cruel way of controlling the fox population.

Shooting bears and deer is popular in North America. Small songbirds are shot on migration in Mediterranean countries with no controls at all. Ducks, geese, grouse, pheasant, foxes and stags are all hunted and killed in Britain.

Slaughter of the dolphins

In 1988 an American environmentalist called Sam LaBudde took a job as cook on a Mexican fishing boat. He took a video camera with him, and for four months recorded the slaughter of dolphins during the tuna fishing season. Tuna fishermen in the eastern Pacific look for schools of dolphins, to give them an idea of where to place their nets: tuna swim below dolphins, possibly because they share the same prey. When a school of dolphins is spotted, speedboats are launched to chase them until they are exhausted. Then the fishermen run a long net which surrounds both dolphins and tuna. The dolphins are usually drowned in the nets. Official figures say that 120,000 dolphins are killed each year in this callous way. The true figure may be nearer 250,000. In one catch that Sam LaBudde recorded, 200 dolphin were drowned and only one tuna was caught.

Japanese fishermen catch salmon in the North Pacific by hanging nets in the sea. The nets are too fine for dolphins to detect with their sonar, and many thousands are drowned each year when they become entangled.

The Faroe Islands bloodbath
Pilot whales, which are a type of dolphin, are regularly slaughtered in large numbers in the Faroe Islands, in a traditional bloodbath in which they are hacked to death by hand. Once, the meat was essential to keep the islanders alive through the winter. Now most of it is thrown out to rot, but the cruel pastime goes on.

POINTLESS SLAUGHTER — 2

Saving the Innocent

Sam LaBudde's videotape drew attention to the horrific massacre of the dolphins. It was used in a campaign to show what happened during tuna fishing, and people were shocked when they saw it. At the same time, scientists published figures showing that in the 25 years since this method of fishing began, about 6 million dolphins, and at least four species of whale, had also been trapped.

Fishing fleets from the USA were largely responsible for the deaths until the early 1970s, when the US Government passed the Marine Mammal Protection Act. Part of this stated that no dolphins should be killed during tuna fishing. American fishermen now use nets that can be sunk below the dolphins allowing them to escape but trapping the tuna fish. However, well over 20,000 dolphins are still killed each year.

The USA has said that if other countries want to sell their tuna to them, they must make sure that they kill no more dolphins than the US fishing fleet. To get around this, these countries sell their tuna elsewhere. Mexico sells 83 per cent of its catch to countries in the European Community. Environmentalists have put pressure on the EC to ban imports of this tuna, but success may be far off. Nonetheless, their efforts have drawn attention to the needless slaughter of dolphins, and as a result many people have decided not to eat tuna at all.

Hunting

There are people in several countries who campaign to stop blood sports, such as fox and stag hunting, hare coursing and badger baiting. In Britain, they might belong to the League Against Cruel Sports. Sometimes their protests lead to fights with the hunters, with resulting bad publicity. But their campaigns have led the hunters to make sure that the animals die with the least possible suffering.

Big-game hunting declined rapidly after the Second World War, which ended in 1945. The main reason was that the countries where the animals lived passed laws forbidding any more killing. Public opinion changed quickly, perhaps because of the popularity of television wildlife programmes, which showed the beauty and excitement of wild animals and places.

Project Tiger

The first accurate count of tigers was made by the Indian Forest Service in 1972 in preparation for Project Tiger. This was one of the first major conservation projects of the World Wildlife Fund (now known as the Worldwide Fund for Nature). The survey discovered the shocking fact that only 1,827 tigers were left alive. The rest had been hunted and killed. Estimates for Bangladesh and Nepal added only about 350 to the total number of tigers left. The World Wildlife Fund enlisted the help of the governments of all three countries. Soon laws were made to protect tigers, as well as the many other species that make up the food chain of which the tiger is the top. Eight large nature reserves were set up and a budget of £3.25 million was allocated for the work. Now the tiger is safe, and the reserves attract large numbers of visitors. The money the visitors pay helps to maintain the reserves and finance further research on tigers and their prey.

Right A radio collar being fitted to a female tiger in Nepal. She has been drugged, but will not suffer harm.

Many people were shocked by Sam LaBudde's video showing the unnecessary slaughter of dolphins by Pacific tuna fishermen.

What you can do
When you buy tuna, ask the manager of the shop where it comes from. If he or she doesn't know, write to the head buyer of the supermarket chain and ask again. If the tuna comes from the Pacific, refuse to buy it.

POLLUTING THE PLANET — 1

Pollution and Acid Rain

Fields of crops are not natural, because they consist of large numbers of one single species of plant — wheat, for example. In a natural environment, many species would grow together. Because of this specialization, the crops are liable to be attacked by insects, which can breed in enormous numbers and destroy the entire crop. To prevent this, farmers use pesticides: chemicals that kill the pests.

Poisonous pesticides

If used in large enough doses, many pesticides are poisonous to other forms of life as well as to the insect pests. They also last a long time, breaking down only very slowly into harmless substances. If a small bird eats beetles that have been poisoned with one of these persistent pesticides, the poison does not pass out of the bird's body, but accumulates in its body fat. By the time the small bird is eaten, perhaps by a bird of prey, it will contain a strong dose of the poison, enough to kill the predator or to interfere with its breeding.

Pesticides that are washed off farmland by rain and then pass into rivers eventually accumulate in the bodies of fish. They go on to harm animals higher up the food chain, such as otters, long after

Right Pesticides sprayed on plants pass up the food chain, and eventually the poison reaches the creatures at the top of the chain.

Acid rain damage was first noticed in 1970 in the Black Forest, Germany. By 1984 more than half of the country's forests were damaged.

the fields were sprayed. One persistent pesticide, DDT, has been found in the fat of penguins in the Antarctic, thousands of kilometres from where it was first used.

Acid rain

Another major type of chemical pollution is acid rain. It is formed from the sulphur dioxide and nitrogen oxides which are produced by burning fossil fuels, such as coal, oil and gas. Vehicle exhaust emissions also contribute to acid rain. When these products meet damp air they form acids which eventually fall to the ground as rain.

Acid rain kills fish and trees. In many lakes and rivers in Canada and Scandinavia, rain has made the water so acid that nothing can live in it. Predators that depended on the fish for food must leave or die out. The damage caused by acid rain was first seen in the forests of West Germany in the early 1970s. It is now a major problem in North America and Europe, and is also spreading to South America, parts of Africa, and Asia.

POLLUTING THE PLANET — 2

Fighting Pollution

The worst of the harmful pesticides are now banned, though their effects will be felt for a long time. Alternative pesticides are being developed, and they are strictly tested before being let loose on the environment.

A natural insecticide is found in an African plant called *Pyrethrum*. An extract of this, called pyrethrin, is used in some flysprays. It kills insects but is harmless to other forms of life. Greenfly can be controlled by spraying with soapy water instead of pesticide.

Reducing acid rain

The control of acid rain is not so easy as changing pesticides. The Scandinavian countries tried to neutralize the acid by putting lime into their lakes and waterways, but it worked for only a short time. As an even more desperate measure, they tried dropping powdered lime into the forests from aircraft. This was very costly but it showed results.

Main picture Lime is sprayed into an acidified lake in an attempt to neutralize the acid pollution. Unfortunately, this type of treatment works for only a short time and the acidity soon starts to rise again.

However, as soon as the treatment was stopped, the trees once again showed signs of the effects of acidity.

The worst damage to forests from acid rain is in the Netherlands. In places, acid rain has washed so much calcium out of the soil that caterpillars feeding on leaves growing there contain much less calcium than normal. When birds eat the caterpillars, they do not get enough calcium to make proper shells for their eggs. As a result the embryos inside the eggs die. Adding lime to the soil can preserve much more than just the trees. All the animals and plants in the forest will be helped in some way.

Clearly, the problem is very serious. The worst affected countries have suggested that the only answer is for the offending countries to reduce the amount of sulphur and nitrogen in smoke from power stations and vehicle exhausts.

This can be done quite simply but it is expensive. Unfortunately some of the worst offenders are countries in Eastern Europe, such as Poland and East Germany, which have little money to spare for cleaning their smoke. Another difficulty is that acid rain affects other countries, not necessarily those that produce it, so that the 'exporters' of pollution are being asked to spend money to help the 'importers', not their own people. There might have to be a change in international law before the offenders can be forced to stop polluting the air.

What you can do
If you must use flysprays, buy those with pyrethrin as the poison in them. Better still, think of 'green' ways of controlling insect pests. Persuade people you know to use unleaded petrol, and don't drop litter.

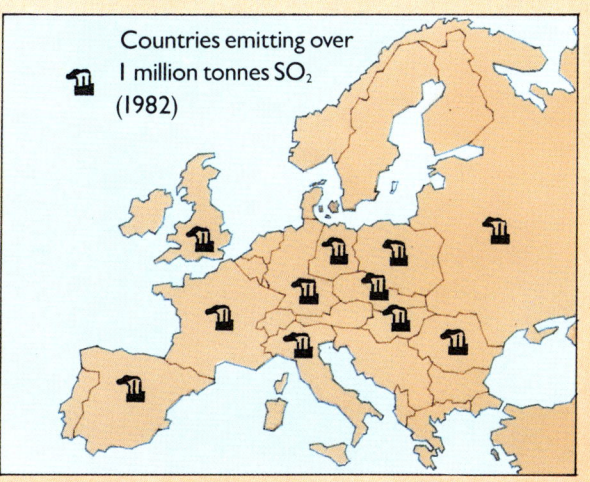

Countries emitting over 1 million tonnes SO₂ (1982)

Who cares?
Most European countries are taking action to limit the damage caused by sulphur dioxide (SO$_2$) pollution from their industrial sites. Their plans are as follows: France and Luxembourg — reduction by at least 50% by 1990; Italy, USSR, Czechoslovakia, Hungary and East Germany — 30% cut by 1993; Finland and West Germany — 50-65% cut by 1993; Norway — 50% cut by 1994; Austria — 70% cut by 1994; Sweden, Switzerland, Denmark, Netherlands and Belgium — 50-68% cut by 1995. Spain, Great Britain, Greece, Poland, Romania and Yugoslavia have made no commitment to reduce emissions in the forseeable future.

RAINFORESTS — 1

Rainforest Destruction

The tropical rainforests are important, not only to wildlife but to the human race as well. The roots of the forest trees hold the soil in place, preventing erosion. The soil stores water, filtering and slowly releasing it so that clean rivers flow steadily out of the forests. And the trees themselves have an effect on the climate, gathering clouds that either produce rain or condense on the leaves like dew. In spite of this, people are destroying the rainforests at an alarming rate.

Slash and burn
The Amazon rainforest makes up almost two-thirds of the world's total area of rainforest. In 1987, 204,000 sq. km of the rainforest were burned to clear land for agriculture. In 1988, the figure was

Clearing rainforest for agriculture produces soil which is fertile for only a very short time. When its nutrients have been used up, the soil is useless for growing crops.

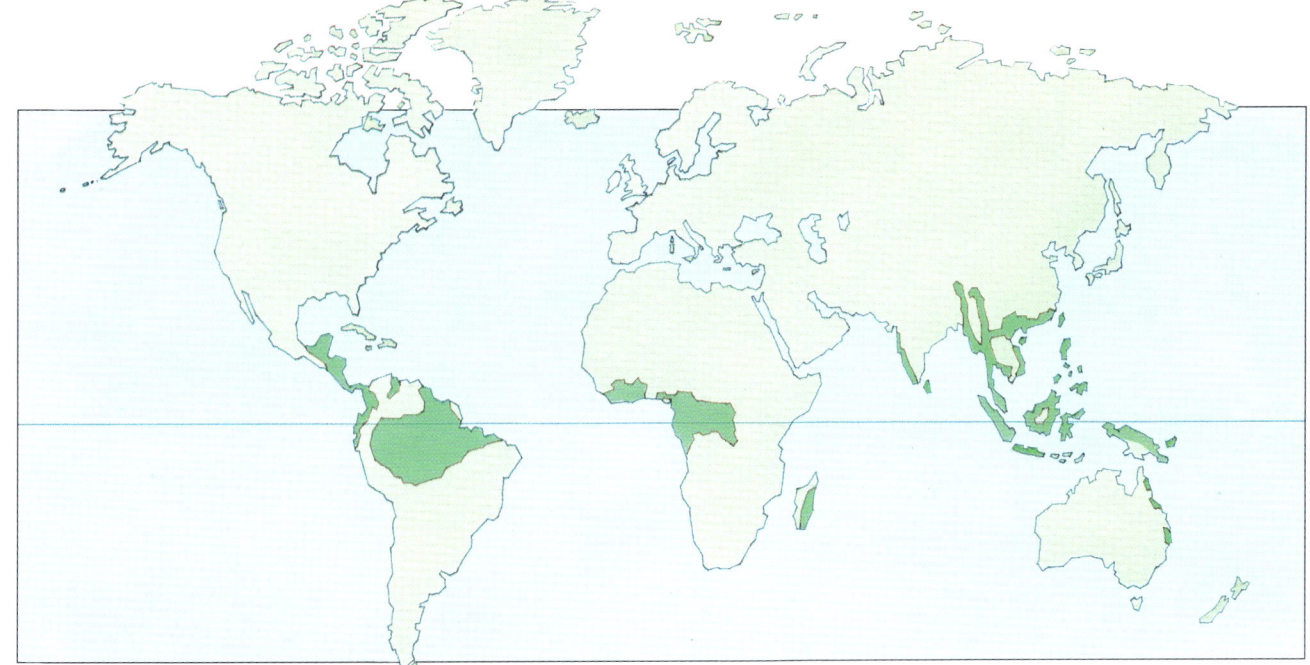

Above The world's rainforests lie in a narrow band in the tropics, north and south of the equator. They grow in areas where the climate is hot all year round and the rainfall is very high. The largest rainforest is in the Amazon Basin in South America.

slightly smaller, about 121,000 sq. km, of which 48,000 sq. km was virgin rainforest. About the same amount again was damaged or destroyed by felling trees for timber and by building dams. These figures are only for the Amazon; in the whole world the area of forest which is damaged or destroyed every year would cover most of Australia.

The effect of this destruction on the climate and the land itself is very serious and permanent; but the effect on the wildlife is devastating.

Among the most endangered animals are the primates, which depend entirely on the forest for a home. The woolly spider monkey is the first primate to die out when rainforest is disturbed; there are just 100 left alive in Brazil. The orang utan lives in Sumatra, where there may be as many as 2,000 in nature reserves. Another 2,000 live outside the reserves, but their chances of survival are small because of the rate at which the forest is being cut down. The same story could be told for hundreds of other harmless and beautiful animals.

Species lost for ever
The rainforest contains a greater number and variety of plant and animal species than any other habitat on earth. Many are still unknown to science. By the year 2000, one million species will have disappeared, many of them before they have even been discovered.

RAINFORESTS — 2

Preserving the Rainforests

The most obvious products of the rainforest are the huge trees, which provide valuable hardwoods for building and furniture. However, when the trees are chopped down and removed, other forest products — crops such as fruits and nuts, and renewable resources such as rubber — cease to exist. Yet these 'non-wood products' are worth nearly ten times as much as the timber and, unlike the timber, they grow back again when they are harvested.

However, the timber earns money, for governments and for large international companies. The grasslands that remain when the trees have gone can be used for ranching cattle. While the non-wood products support a living for many people, they earn little or no money for the country as a whole.

Thanks to the efforts of the Brazilian campaigner Chico Mendez and others like him, people now realize that developing the rainforests for timber and cattle creates serious problems. Although it may make money for governments, it also causes unemployment and homelessness for people who lived in the forests, as well as destroying wildlife.

Agroforestry

Instead of cutting down any more rainforest, Brazil might try agroforestry, in which crops are grown with the forest, not instead of it. Crops are chosen which will grow well in forest clearings, without any need to cut down more trees. The crops, which include mangoes, citrus fruits and yucca, provide a living for the local population and the rainforest trees and plants are preserved.

Wood for fuel and building can be provided by planting new trees where the old ones have been cut down. But if we wish to preserve the remaining rainforests, we must learn to do without the ancient hardwoods for building and furniture-making. They are very beautiful and valuable as timber, but they are even more beautiful and valuable as forests.

Main picture Agroforestry involves planting crops in small clearings in the rainforest.

The work of Chico Mendez

A rubber tapper called Chico Mendez realized the value of the forest to ordinary farmers and forest workers in Brazil. He wanted large areas to be left standing, so that people could continue to extract the products that were their livelihood. But the commercial cattle ranchers disagreed with his arguments. On 22 December 1988, the cattle ranchers shot him dead. His death did not silence his arguments: instead they were heard all over the world.

Right Mendez addressing a protest meeting.

What you can do
Use recycled paper whenever you can. Do not buy articles made from tropical hardwoods such as teak, mahogany and ebony. Support one of the many organizations that are working to save the forests.

If the destruction of the rainforests can be halted, the way of life of forest-dwellers like these Amazon Indians may be protected.

WETLANDS UNDER THREAT — 1

Vanishing Wetlands

Wetlands are places which are neither land nor water. Coastal marshes and river estuaries, mangrove swamps and inland bogs are all practically worthless to human beings but vital to the plants and animals that make their homes in them. Wetlands cover 6 per cent of the earth's surface. They are threatened because people drain the water from them to make them useful for agriculture or building.

Wetlands are very productive. Although few species can live in an estuary, for example, those that can survive the daily changes between fresh and salt water live there in huge numbers. Ragworms and shellfish provide food for flocks of migrating shorebirds, and the grasses and other plants on the saltmarshes are eaten by geese.

Mangrove swamps are the main breeding ground for many fish and shellfish, as well as specialized birds and insects. They are important to people, too: they slow down storm surges and tidal waves, which would otherwise cause serious floods inland. In Bangladesh most of the mangrove trees that once grew at the mouth of the River Ganges have now gone, and storms regularly cause floods which make thousands of people homeless.

Nurseries for fish

The Waddenzee, along the coast of the Netherlands, produces 60 per cent of the shrimps in the North Sea. In the USA, 70 per cent of the fish and shellfish that Americans eat depend on wetlands for food and breeding grounds. Before people realized the importance of these apparently

The wetlands in Florida, USA, support a variety of animals, including those in the picture.
Key: 1. Green heron; 2. Black legged common egret; 3. Wood ibis; 4. White ibis; 5. Blue heron; 6. Grey necked heron; 7. Alligator.

Draining wetlands destroys the habitats of many native species as well as migratory birds.

useless areas, more than half of the wetlands in the USA had been destroyed, mostly by drainage.

Apart from draining them to 'reclaim' the land, people interfere with wetlands by dredging the rivers that flow through them, so that the silt is washed away. Building sea walls to protect the land beside an estuary removes the sloping foreshore where birds like to feed.

WETLANDS UNDER THREAT — 2

Protecting Wetlands

The fight to save the world's wetlands really began in 1971, at a meeting at Ramsar, in Iran. A Convention was drawn up in which countries agreed to make a list of their most important wetlands and to help each other protect them. Twenty-three countries were represented at the meeting. Since then, the number of members has grown to 54, and between them they have listed 421 places to be protected all over the world, covering more than 22 million hectares.

The Ramsar Convention was a great step forward, but there is still a long way to go before all the remaining wetlands in the world are safe.

The Camargue

A fine example of a protected wetland is the Regional Park of Camargue, at the mouth of the River Rhône in southern France. It covers over 850 sq. km of sandy soil, marshes and shallow lakes, with a patchwork of grassland and scrub between the waterways. Wide sand dunes along the shore support clumps of juniper and pine, and the beach stretches for over 100 km.

The Camargue is famous for its wild horses and cattle, as well as the beauties of the scenery. But above all it is noted for its birdlife. It is one of the

Above The Camargue, in southern France, is one of the three most important wetlands in Europe, and is now protected by law.

Left Migrant winter flocks gather in vast numbers on the Wildfowl and Wetlands Trust site at Welney, in Britain.

three most important wetlands in Europe, the breeding place of flamingos, herons, ducks, bee-eaters and many other birds. It is a vital resting place for migrating birds: over 300 different species have been seen, often in very large flocks.

To protect the area further, there is a State Nature Reserve in the middle of the Park, which is even more carefully controlled. Its 13,000 hectares are open only to people who can prove that they have a special reason for being there, usually biologists. Two research centres produce a vast amount of information about the area, especially its birdlife.

However, the Camargue does have its problems. It is an important rice-growing area, producing 100,000 tonnes per year. Rice is grown under water and the rice fields drain into the central reserve, causing changes in the depth and saltiness of the water. Sometimes pesticides leak into the reserve, along with industrial pollution from the river; and many campers and tourists leave rubbish along the beaches.

What you can do
Visit the Wildfowl and Wetlands Trust at one of its many branches in Britain. Keep an eye on local builders and farmers. If they are planning to drain ponds or dredge streams, write to your local paper about it.

ENDANGERED PLANTS — 1

Plants under Threat

The risk to wildlife includes not only animals of all kinds, but plants, too. Pollution and habitat destruction kill plants as well as animals, and some plants have become very rare as a result. They, too, need to be protected. The number of plant species in danger of extinction by the year 2000 is estimated to be between 25,000 and 40,000.

Rare plant collectors
Some plants are caught in the 'rarity trap'. They become famous because of their rarity, the demand for them by collectors makes them valuable, so that more are collected, and they become rarer still. Some wild orchids may have become extinct because of their popularity with collectors. The trade in protected plants is illegal. The white nun orchid, from Central America, is listed in CITES Appendix I (see page 20), and another orchid, *Drymodes picta* from Burma, is also extremely rare because of over-collection. Both plants are still collected wherever they can be found, and smuggled to the people who want to buy them. Sadly, both are very difficult, if not impossible, to breed away from their native forests. Orchid collectors in the USA alone import 50,000 of these plants yearly. About 70 per cent come from Thailand, and most are believed to be collected from the wild and smuggled out of the country.

Cacti from North America and southern Africa, and South African cycads — palm-like plants which have not changed for more than 50 million years — are all being caught in the same rarity trap, and are in real danger of extinction.

Losing our common flowers
Other plants are lost because they are considered to be weeds. The corn cockle, a pretty blue flower which used to grow commonly in grain fields all over Britain, is now found in only three counties. This is partly because of the use of weedkillers, and partly because modern methods of cleaning crop seeds remove the seeds of the corn cockle from the

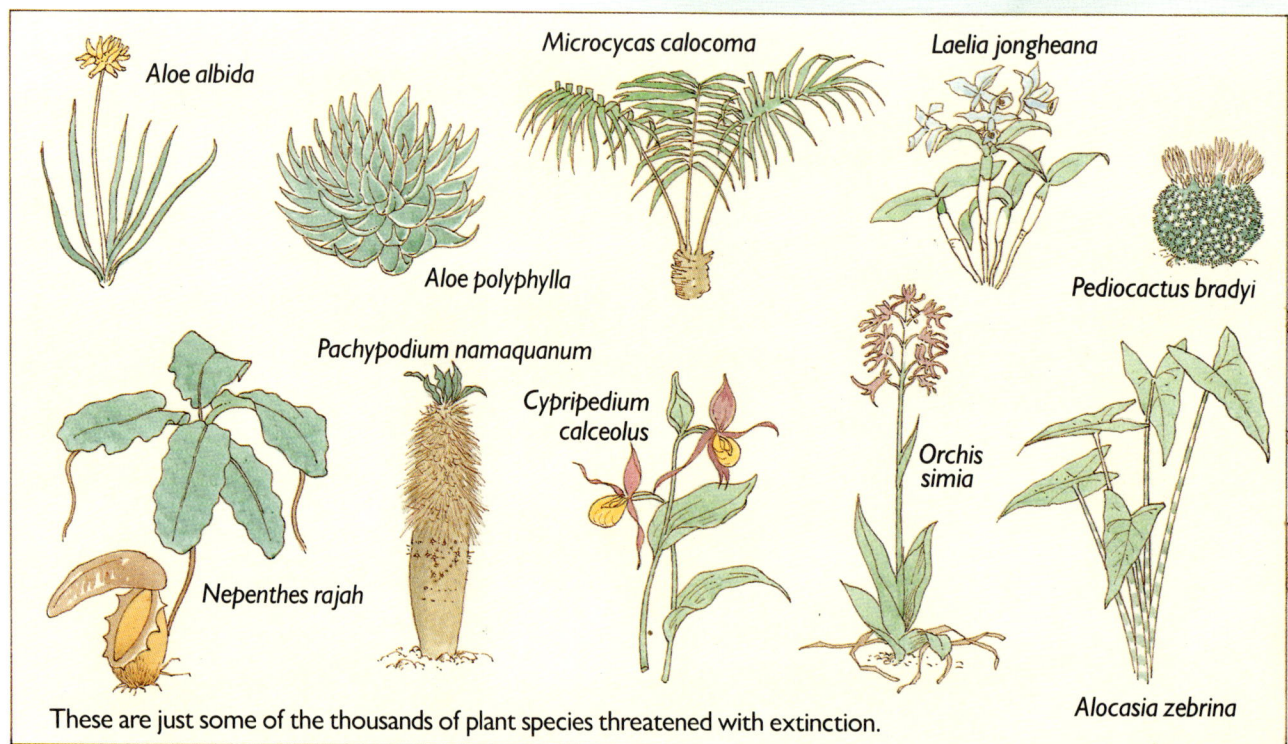

These are just some of the thousands of plant species threatened with extinction.

38

mixture. Cowslips are now protected by law in Britain. They became rare because people dug them up to plant in their own gardens, and also because of the use of weedkillers to 'improve' pasture. Some plants are poisonous to cattle and other grazing animals, and they too may be threatened with extinction.

So many *Rafflesia arnoldi* have been taken from the wild that it is now almost extinct.

ENDANGERED PLANTS — 2

Planting the Future

Some of the exotic plants that people keep in pots in their houses are rare in their native land. African violets, for example, are much more common in Europe than in their native Africa. They have been over-collected in Africa but survive in Europe because they are cultivated by commercial growers. This gives us a clue to a way of protecting rare plant species.

The Madagascar Periwinkle
The chemicals that make some plants poisonous may be valuable if they are properly understood and used. The Madagascar Periwinkle is a very good example. A drug made from this little pink-flowered plant is now used all over the world to treat a type of cancer called leukaemia, saving many children's lives.

This is an area of protected rainforest in Costa Rica. Rainforests may contain medicinal plants which are still unknown to science — another reason why they should be saved.

A scientist at a plant research laboratory. Research into the production of new species of crop plants and the preservation of seeds in seed banks may offer hope for the future.

Growing in a controlled environment

Plants that have become rare because of over-collecting or because their habitat has been reduced or destroyed, can be gathered and grown in carefully controlled conditions, until they can be replanted in their native land. The International Organization for Succulent Plant Study has found ways of growing rare cacti for collectors, so that they need not buy endangered plants that have been taken from the deserts of North America and southern Africa.

However, this does not always work. Crocuses are easy to grow and cheap to buy in garden centres; but there is still a steady trade in bulbs collected from the wild, especially in Turkey, which has the greatest variety in the world. In 1988, Turkey exported 22 million wild crocus bulbs to the Netherlands. Some conservationists think that crocuses should be put on CITES Appendix II, but the Dutch members are unlikely to agree because bulb-growing is such an important business in the Netherlands.

Because some orchids are so difficult to grow in temperate countries, the only way to protect the rarest species is to refuse to buy them, even in the tropical countries where they grow naturally.

It might seem strange that crop plants could be in danger, but they are. Wheat, for example, is a giant grass with huge seeds, which has been bred from a small wild plant. Intensive breeding methods often reduce a plant's natural resistance to pests and diseases. In Europe and North America, most varieties of wheat last for only about ten years, before their enemies overcome them and they become useless as crops. The same happens to other cultivated crop plants. To protect them, and the people who need to eat them, it is important to keep a store of seeds from wild plants. In this way new varieties can be bred with better resistance to disease.

Seed banks

Seeds can last for a very long time if they are stored in the right conditions. Seeds from an Indian lotus plant were recently dug up from the bed of a lake which had dried out over a thousand years ago. Despite being buried for all this time, the seeds germinated perfectly. With modern methods of storage, it should be possible to keep 'banks' of seeds for a very long time, until it is safe to replant them in their proper habitat.

The best way to protect plants applies equally well to animals. We must make sure that their habitat remains safe for ever.

> **What you can do**
> Do not buy orchids. If there were no trade in them, they would not be collected. Do not pick or dig up wild plants when you go on country walks. Plant wild flower seeds (available from most garden centres) in your garden.

Glossary

Acid rain Rain containing sulphuric and nitric acids, formed when sulphur dioxide and nitrogen oxides combine with water droplets in the air.
Ambergris A strong-smelling waxy substance found in the stomach of sperm whales.
Baleen The filter plates in the mouth of some whales, used for catching their food.
Bird of prey A hunting bird, such as an eagle or a hawk.
Commercial Done to make a profit.
Condensation When water cools and changes from a gas to a liquid.
Crop plants Plants which are grown to be harvested and then eaten or used in industry.
Cull The killing of a number of animals in a herd or group.
Cultivated Grown on purpose, not wild.
Dominant Most successful.
Environment The surroundings of a plant or animal.
Erosion The wearing away of the land by rain, rivers or wind.
Estuaries Places where rivers widen out and flow into the sea.
European Community (EC) A union of European countries formed in 1957. There are now twelve members: Belgium, France, Italy, Luxembourg, the Netherlands, West Germany, Denmark, the Republic of Ireland, Britain, Spain, Portugal and Greece.
Exotic Coming from another country.
Extinction The death of an entire species of plant or animal.
Food chain A sequence in which plants are eaten by small animals which are eaten by larger animals, and so on.
Fossil fuels Fuels that were made from the decay of ancient plants: coal, oil and natural gas.
Germinate To develop shoots and grow.
Habitat The place where an animal or plant lives naturally.
Hardwood The wood of a broadleaved tree, including oak, beech, mahogany and teak.
Harpoon A sharp missile attached to a long cord and fired from a gun when hunting whales.
Lime A compound of calcium which is used to neutralize acids.
Maharajah An Indian prince.
Mammals Warm-blooded animals which feed their young on milk produced by the mother.

Mangrove A tropical evergreen tree or shrub often with long aerial roots. Mangroves grow in dense thickets along coasts.
Migration The regular, seasonal movement of animals from one climate to another.
National Park An area of land controlled by a government to preserve its natural beauty.
Neutralize To make a liquid less acid.
Omnivorous Able to eat both animals and plants.
Overfishing Catching fish faster than they are able to breed, so that their numbers are steadily reduced.
Persistent Long-lasting.
Pesticide A chemical used to kill animal pests.
Pitfall A trap made by digging a hole in the ground and hiding it with branches and leaves.
Predator An animal that hunts other animals for food.
Pollution The spoiling of the environment with harmful substances.
Prey An animal that is hunted by another animal.
Primates The highest order of animals. Monkeys, apes and humans are all primates.
Quarry The prey of a hunter.
Rainforest An area of dense, tropical forest.
Rubber tapper Someone who collects the sap of rubber trees to be made into rubber.
School A group of whales, dolphins or porpoises.
Silt Mud made of very small particles.
Sonar Sensing the surroundings by listening for echoes of sounds. Whales and dolphins use sonar.
Species A group of living things which are alike and are able to breed with each other. All human being belong to the same species.
Temperate A word describing the mild climate in parts of the world between the tropics and the polar regions.
Tropical A word describing the hot, wet climate in parts of the world between the tropics, on either side of the equator.
Tuna A large ocean-living fish, caught as food for humans.
Virgin Untouched.
Virus A tiny organism which multiplies inside a plant or the body of an animal causing disease.
Watercourse Any channel of water, such as a ditch, stream, river or canal.

Further Information

If you want to find out more about wildlife and the organizations that are working to protect it, you might like to read some of the books below and contact the conservation groups at the addresses listed here.

Useful addresses

Australia:
   Australian Conservation Foundation
   GPO Box 1875, Canberra ACT 2601

   Friends of the Earth
   366 Smith Street, Collingwood VIC 3066

   Greenpeace
   785 George Street, Sydney NSW 2000

Britain:
   Friends of the Earth
   26-28 Underwood Street, London N1 7JQ

   Greenpeace
   30-31 Islington Green, London N1 8XE

   International Centre for Conservation Education
   Greenfield House, Guiting Power
   Cheltenham, Glos GL54 5TZ

   International Council for Bird Preservation
   32 Cambridge Road, Girton, Cambridge
   CB3 0PJ

   International Fund for Animal Welfare
   Tubwell House, New Road, Crowborough
   East Sussex TN6 2QH

   Lynx
   PO Box 509, Dunmow, Essex CM6 1UH

   Royal Society for Nature Conservation
   The Green, Nettleham, Lincoln LN2 2NR

   Royal Society for the Protection of Birds
   The Lodge, Sandy, Bedfordshire SG19 2DL

   The Wildfowl and Wetlands Trust
   The New Grounds, Slimbridge, Glos GL2 7BT

   Worldwide Fund for Nature
   11-13 Ockford Road, Godalming, Surrey
   GU7 1QU

Canada:
   Greenpeace
   427 Bloor St West, Toronto, Ontario M5S 1X7

   Worldwide Fund for Nature
   60 St Clair Avenue East, Suite 201
   Toronto, Ontario M4T 1N5

New Zealand
   ECO
   PO Box 11057, Wellington

   Greenpeace
   Nagal House, 5th Floor
   Courthouse Lane, Auckland

USA:
   Friends of the Earth
   530 7th Street SE, Washington DC 20003

   Greenpeace
   1436 U Street NW, Washington DC 20009

Other countries:
   United Nations Environment Programme
   PO Box 30552, Nairobi, Kenya

   Greenpeace International
   Keizersgracht 176
   1016 DW Amsterdam, The Netherlands

Books to read

Acid Rain by P. Neal (Dryad, 1985)
The Animal Smugglers by J. Nichol (Christopher Helm, 1987)
Disappearing Mammals by J. Leigh-Pemberton (Ladybird, 1973)
Endangered Animals by M. Penny (Wayland, 1988)
Endangered Wildlife by M. Banks (Wayland, 1987)
Finding Out about Conservation by J. Bentley and B. Charlton (Batsford, 1983)
Pollution and Wildlife by M. Bright (Franklin Watts, 1987)

Index

Acid rain 27, 28-9
Agroforestry 32
Amazon rainforest 30, 31
Ambergris 7
Antarctic 7, 16, 27
Austria 29

Baleen 7
Baltic Sea 11
Bangladesh 24, 34
Bears 14
Belgium 29
Big-game hunting 22, 24
Blood sports 22, 24
Bobcats 14
Brazil 31, 32

Cacti 38
Camargue 36-7
Canada 5, 13, 27
Chinchillas 14
Convention on the International Trade in
    Endangered Species (CITES) 16, 20, 38, 41
Corn cockle 38-9
Costa Rica 40
Cowslips 39
Crocodile farming 21
Crocuses 41
Cycads 38
Czechoslovakia 29

Davies, Brian 12
DDT 27
Denmark 29
Deserts 5, 41
Dolphins 22-4

East Germany 29
Elephants 18-19
    poaching of 19
European Community (EC) 12, 24

Factory ships 6
Faroe Islands 23
Finland 29
Fish farming 13
Food chain 24, 27
Forests, acidified 26, 28-9
Fossey, Dian 20-21
Fox hunting 22

France 29, 36
Fur, fake 16
Fur farming 16-17
Fur trapping 14-15
    protests against 16-17

Ganges, River 34
Gorillas 19, 20-21
    poaching of 19, 21
Great Britain 29, 38, 39
Greece 29
Greenpeace 9

Hardwoods 32, 33
Hong Kong 19
Hungary 29

Iceland 9
India 22, 24
International Fund for Animal Welfare (IFAW) 12, 13
International Organization for Succulent Plant
    Study 41
International Whaling Commission (IWC) 8, 9
Italy 29
Ivory 18, 19

Jaguars 14
Japan 7, 8, 9, 19

Kenya 20

LaBudde, Sam 22-3, 24
Lakes, acidified 27, 28-9
League Against Cruel Sports 24
Lime 28-9
Luxembourg 29
Lynx 16, 17

Madagascar Periwinkle 40
Mendez, Chico 32
Mexico 24
Mink ranching 17

Nature reserves 24, 37
Netherlands 29, 34, 41
Nepal 24
North Sea 11, 34
North Yemen 18
Norway 8, 9, 10, 11

Orang utans 31
Orchids 38, 41
Overfishing 11, 12

Papua, New Guinea 21
Penguins 27
Pesticides 26-7, 28, 37
Plant research laboratories 41
Plants, smuggling of rare 38-9
Poaching 19, 20-21
Poland 29
Pollution 5, 11, 26-7, 37, 38
Population, growth of human 5
Project Tiger 24
Pyrethrin 28, 29

Rafflesia arnoldi 38
Rainforests 30-33
Ramsar Convention, 1971 36
Rhino, black 18, 20
Rhône, River 36
Romania 29
Rwanda 20

Sarguja, Maharajah of 22
Seal hunting 10-11, 12, 13
    protests against 12-13
Seals 10-13
    common 11
    fur 11, 16
    grey 10, 11
    harp 5, 10, 11
    hooded 10
Sealskin 5, 10 11, 12, 13
Seal virus 11
Sea otters 16
Seed banks 41
Spain 29
Sulphur dioxide 27, 29
Sweden 29
Switzerland 29

Thailand 38
Tigers 14, 22, 24
Timber 30, 32
Traps
    gin (leghold) 15
    pitfall 15
    snare 15
Tuna fishing 22-3, 24
Turkey 41

United Nations 8
Unleaded petrol 29
USA 14, 24, 34, 38
USSR 8, 29

Weedkillers 38-39
West Germany 26, 27
Wetlands 34-7
    destruction of 35
Whale products 6, 7
Whales 6-9, 24
    blue 7
    declining numbers of 7
    fin 7
    humpback 7
    minke 6
    pilot 23
    sperm 7

Whaling 6-9
    moratorium 8-9
    protests against 8-9
    quotas 8
    for scientific research 9
Wheat 41
Wildfowl and Wetlands Trust 16, 37
Worldwide Fund for Nature (WWF) 24